HANDLING DIFFICULT PARENTS

Successful Strategies for Educators

Allen N. Mendler, Ph.D.

Discipline Associates

Rochester, New York

Printed in the United States of America

Design by Donna Ratzel

ISBN 0965511502

DEDICATION

To the memory of Raoul Poliakin, master violinist, teacher and mentor for showing me that excellence and achievement comes from passion and effort. Your presence continues to inspire me nearly forty years after my last lesson.

ABOUT THE AUTHOR

Allen N. Mendler, Ph.D., provides seminars and consultation on topics related to teaching and reaching challenging students. His organization, Discipline Associates, helps educators learn how to motivate and handle difficult students, deal effectively with tough parents, provide effective school and classroom discipline, and facilitate successful inclusion. He is a school psychologist, parent, teacher, educational consultant, and seminar leader based in Rochester, New York.

Dr. Mendler has worked extensively with children of all ages in both general and special education settings. His emphasis is on developing effective frameworks and strategies for educators and youth professionals to help difficult students succeed. As the internationally acclaimed co-author of *Discipline with Dignity*, Dr. Mendler has given thousands of workshops and is highly acclaimed as a motivational speaker and trainer. He was presented with the esteemed Crazy Horse Award for courage in reaching disadvantaged youth and recognized for his outstanding teaching, by many organizations including the Bureau of Education and Research. Dr. Mendler is the author or co-author of thirteen books including *Just in Time: Powerful Strategies to Promote Positive Behavior, Connecting with Students*, and *Power Struggles: Successful Techniques for Educators*. His articles have appeared in many journals, including *Educational Leadership, Phi Delta Kappan, Reclaiming Children* and *Youth* and *Reaching Today's Youth*.

Contact the author for training and seminar information at Discipline Associates, P.O. Box 20481, Rochester, New York 14602, (800) 772-4227, or visit the website at www.disciplineassociates.com.

ACKNOWLEDGMENTS

I'd like to thank Nancy Modrak at the Association for Supervision and Curriculum Development and Rhonda Rieseberg at Solution Tree, for their encouraging feedback, helpful suggestions and favorable review. A great big thank you is in order to my dear friend and colleague, Linda Steinberg, who read the manuscript and offered both high praise and a few tips for improvement. As always, my partner and frequent co-author, Rick Curwin, was there to read and critique the work to help make it as beneficial to the lives of educators as possible. I am grateful to the many educators across the country who continue to attend my seminars and invite me to their schools. It is you from whom I continue to learn so that I can share your best practices with others in the form of a practical book. It is my hope that *Handling Difficult Parents* will offer you many effective ways to best respond when your equilibrium is challenged by parents who themselves may be struggling with a variety of life's issues.

It has been a particular source of joy and pride to witness my son and partner, Brian Mendler, take his place as an outstanding educator of children and fellow educators. His sensitivity, insight, creativity and persistence are making differences in the lives of the children he teaches and the educators he mentors. Both they and I are lucky to have him. In addition to Brian, I am blessed to have a growing group of outstanding educators affiliated with Discipline Associates who share their excellence through our organization: Willeta Corbett, Jerry Evanski, Colleen and Dave Zawadzki, Mary Beth Hewitt and Donald Price. Your inspiring message of hope along with lots of practical strategies resonates with educators throughout the country. I also wish to express my appreciation to my helpful and loyal office staff, Tammy Rowland, Heidi Alati and Allison Yauchzee. You are the nuts and bolts that keep things solid. To Lori Erickson, Denise Bodart, Matt Mickelson, and Lynne Peterson at Otter Creek Institute, a big thank you for your on-going support of our work. My deep appreciation to Jeff Jones and staff at Solution Tree for their enthusiasm and interest in collaborating on a variety of worthy projects that benefit educators.

Finally, I want to thank Jason Mendler and Ticia Valle, my loving son and daughter-in-law for recently making me a grandfather of twins, Caleb and Ava, my teenage daughter Lisa Mendler for the daily joy she brings and for keeping me current, and Barbara Mendler, my wife and soul mate who is always there for me through thick and thin.

HANDLING DIFFICULT PARENTS

Successful Strategies for Educators

INTRODUCTION

"Really! We have no problems with him at home."

"I don't understand why you are picking on my kid. But if it doesn't stop, something more will be done."

"My child said that others in the class are doing the same as she, yet she is always the one getting into trouble. Do you just not like my child?

"Luan has never had a problem in school before. I'm not sure that his style of learning is best suited to your style of teaching."

"Johnny just needs a little more attention and then I am sure everything will be fine."

"I don't see how you could possibly have graded that paper a 'C'.

"Billy is very bright. He was in the 99% ile on the last standardized test. I think the problem might be that he is not being sufficiently challenged."

1

There is a cartoon by John McPherson (2004), in which a teacher introduces herself to her class and writes the following on the chalkboard: DON'T LIKE MY TEACHING: CALL 1-800-YOU-FAIL. When I show that cartoon in seminars I teach, it usually gets a hearty laugh. Times have changed. It used to be that most teachers experienced a sense of autonomy fueled by trust so that they did not always have to look over their shoulders with every decision while worrying about how their students or parents would react. Remembering back to my own school days, I was mortified at the thought, much less the action, of a teacher calling home to express concern about behavior. The few times that this occurred led my parents to read me the riot act! Although most parents today are very supportive of teachers and feel good about their child's school, it has become more common for parents to point the finger of blame in the direction of the teacher when their child is having or creating problems. Rather than expecting their child to adapt, problems are attributed to the teacher's lack of sensitivity or poor teaching.

Parents in the lives of teachers are a mixed bag. By and large, they are a blessing. Virtually all of the data on student performance links high achievement and appropriate behavior at school to positive parent involvement in the education of their child. Of particular interest is that high achievement is associated more with parent-child communication at home than with parent involvement at school.

All told, involved parents are crucial for student success. Many become and stay involved in very helpful ways, especially in an era of diminishing resources. In many schools, parent volunteers offer added supervision, mentoring and tutoring. Increasingly, strong PTO's conduct fundraisers to support extracurricular activities otherwise subject to the budget ax.

Sadly, some well-educated parents may actually frown upon teachers whom they view as relatively poorly paid and therefore unworthy of real respect in our highly materialistic society. If their child has a problem at school, it must therefore be due to the teacher. Although most parents appreciate our efforts, few truly understand the energy required to teach. Many parents, themselves overwhelmed by the stresses of life, have little patience for hearing about problems from their children or about their children. It is increasingly common for many to react with defensiveness and anger when we express our concerns, and they are quick to blame us when their children complain to them about a perceived teacher injustice. Many take their complaints right to Administration, completely bypassing the teacher. They may not understand or perhaps it is that they are not particularly sensitive to the fact that their child is one of many students in our class and that our job is to teach all students, not just their child. Worse, a fair number of difficult parents seem insensitive to the havoc caused by their child to everyone else's opportunity to learn. Some parents are literally difficult to reach because of their absence and lack of involvement in their child's life. The bottom line, as all educators who have been in the classroom for more than a few months come to realize, is that parents are a constituency with whom to be reckoned. In fact, a MetLife Survey (2004) found that 31% of all teachers identified "involving parents and communicating with them" as the biggest challenge they face. Fully 73% of new teachers said "too many parents treat school and teachers as adversaries."

WHY ARE PARENTS DIFFICULT?

This book is about how to prevent problems with difficult parents and how to intervene effectively when they blame, complain, argue, or even worse, they don't participate in their child's life. Although there is no rose garden, there are many things that can be done to dramatically increase the odds of teachers gaining parental cooperation, positive involvement, respectful interaction and most important, a strong alliance to benefit students.

Although each situation has its unique set of circumstances, there are six distinguishing factors that can best help us understand the motivations of difficult parents. A description of each factor follows along with practical implications for educators.

A. THEY HAVE A DIFFERENT WAY OF SEEING THINGS

Some parents may not agree with the procedures and practices that you have established in your classroom. It can be very frustrating when parents believe the teacher is doing things that they think fails to bring out the best in their child. From grading practices to seating arrangements, all teachers have to make hundreds of decisions each day and are therefore subject to all kinds of Monday

morning quarterbacking. I recall the annoyance I felt with my daughter's third grade teacher who had implemented a classroom color-coded behavioral system that enabled all students to earn rewards or lose privileges. While my daughter was usually a compliant child who often gained additional rewards, I did not think it was necessary for her to be rewarded for "good" behavior. She already knew that "good" behavior was expected, and using rewards to encourage more of what she could already do automatically, was a little like rewarding crawling in a child who has already mastered running. Further, my extensive study of rewards led me a long time ago to conclude that rewarding children for behaviors they have already mastered tends to diminish intrinsic motivation and lead to feelings of entitlement. Although I chose not to challenge this practice (I mostly loved what this teacher did and how she was), it was my belief that the system did little to teach my daughter about responsibility. Although this teacher probably valued the importance of promoting responsibility in children, my guess is that her concerns about classroom management were more prominent and therefore guided her decision-making. Obviously, a parent's child is his only concern, whereas a teacher has to think about the needs of several students simultaneously.

The different roles can easily lead to different perspectives and the valuing of different priorities. Although it is impossible to make all parents happy, the wise teacher looks for opportunities to invite parental input about classroom practices before problems arise. She establishes practices such as an early year conference or phone call that lets parents know about guidelines and expectations while encouraging parents to tell what they think their child needs from the teacher to be successful.

B. RIGHTLY OR WRONGLY, THEY BELIEVE THE TEACHER DOES NOT CARE ABOUT THEIR CHILD

Some of our students are harder to like than others. In fact, our difficult students often go out of their way to make themselves appear as behaviorally unattractive and unappealing as possible. Making matters worse is that these students always seem present. Students are most often difficult when one or more of their basic life needs is not being fulfilled. In an effort to feel more connected to others, it is common for some to do a lot of irritating things to get noticed. When they believe they will be unsuccessful, some act out or become unmotivated. Further, most become disruptive within the classroom and therefore difficult to like. In fact, it becomes common for them

to provoke the teacher so that the teacher will act mean and unfair. The student may then go home and tells her parent(s) just how mean and unfair the teacher is. As an adult, it requires a great deal of professionalism to set aside personal likes and dislikes. Yet unless we do, we can wind up communicating in a way that makes us appear as mean-spirited people who are out to get the child. Try to remember that on "company time" it is each educator's obligation to teach, reach and motivate every child despite personal preferences. We must also force ourselves to remember that professionalism calls for the respectful and dignified treatment of all parents, including those who may be irritating and obnoxious.

C. THEY DISLIKED SCHOOL AND MAY HARBOR RESENTMENT

Most students who struggle in school have parents that experienced similar struggles. Like their child, these parents often had a school experience that was connected to feelings of failure and/or discomfort. As a result, they are often on-guard and defensive to the basic sights, sounds and smells of school. These parents want to stay as far away as they can. When their children struggle, they can quickly become angry and defensive. They are usually hyper-vigilant to perceived injustice and discrimination, and quick to blame or attack. If the parent is home during the school day when the phone rings, waves of dread in anticipation of bad school news are common. Dread rapidly turns to anger when their fears are confirmed. Since a successful school experience is so dependent upon positive parent support, the challenge is to help these parents create a different picture of school from the one they expect. While conducting training I sometimes ask parents and teachers to remember a time at school when they started out feeling negative but wound up feeling positive. Try this. Maybe you initially thought the teacher was mean or the subject was too hard. Maybe you felt uncomfortable around the other kids. Maybe you lacked confidence at first. Maybe it was something else entirely. It can help to think of a subject that you started out hating when you were at school but wound up loving. What turned things around for you? How did the teacher help change your attitude? The goal is to try to bring behaviors like these to your interactions with students and their parents on a regular basis so that they can begin to get a different picture of what school can be.

D. THEY ARE STRUGGLING TO RAISE THEIR CHILDREN IN A COMPLEX WORLD AND ARE HAVING LIMITED INFLUENCE

There are a myriad of influences that affect our youth including the bombardment of media images and messages, easy availability of drugs and alcohol, gangs, violence, peers and on and on. As a professional, I know these issues well, but at a personal level, these create never-ending struggles and challenges as I raise my teenage daughter. When around her friends, the "uniform" includes the right label jeans and straightened hair. I marvel at how much time she spends each morning checking and re-checking herself to make sure that not a hair is out of place. Although she finds ways of doing well at school, I often wonder how much better she could be doing if she spent more time reading and less time instant messaging. For parents, it takes a lot of time, energy, love and limit-setting to maintain influence. A combination of child temperament and parental frustration can reduce the impact of parents on shaping their child's behavior. For example, some parents get to a point of utter exasperation with their child who refuses to do homework or value school sufficiently to care about getting good grades. Rather than constantly battling, some eventually back off in an effort to preserve their relationship. When educators contact them about a school concern, their feelings of helplessness are often expressed as frustration and anger towards us. Children nowadays can be utterly determined in pressing and nagging their parents for what they want. One informal survey of teenagers found that when they crave something new, most expect to ask nine times before their parents give in. Educators need to understand and express our understanding of the difficulties parents are likely facing so that we can form an alliance with them to help their child by learning how to set and enforce limits. Our suggestions are more likely to be greeted with appreciation when parents sense that teachers understand the challenges they face.

E. THEY DO NOT VALUE OR CANNOT VALUE THE IMPORTANCE OF SCHOOL

Traditionally and historically, immigrants to this country came to quickly realize that the road to a better life was through education. Sacrificing for the next generation was more palatable knowing that the toil and sweat of entry level jobs that few else wanted would probably pay off for their children. Most still believe this. However, even some with good intentions who value the impor-

tance of a good education for their children, are unable to provide the necessary stability because of their preoccupation with survival. If a family must move several times in search of survival, it will be difficult at best for children to succeed in school. Migrant children have a much harder time achieving school success despite a strong family work ethic. Although education may be valued, the reality of providing for more basic needs takes precedent. Despite the greatness of our country, we have helped to create a permanent underclass in America which is disproportionately populated by under-educated African-Americans.

It can be difficult to convey the importance of high standards and high academic achievement when children see little evidence of its presence around them. It is difficult to celebrate the progress that a special education student is making when his parent(s) may be worried about losing social security support if the child becomes unlabeled. The goal is to make school a very welcoming place for parents to come so they will want their children to be there. This requires considerable reaching out to the communities in which we teach so that we become sensitized to their social and cultural mores while at the same time leading the way towards making our schools hopeful places where students can succeed both at school and in life.

F. THEY ARE ANGRY PEOPLE AND SCHOOL IS JUST ONE MORE PLACE TO EXPRESS THEIR OWN UNHAPPINESS

Some people seem to be born miserable and it is a continuous struggle for them to see the bright side of the moment, while others are born with an unflagging optimism that puts sparkle into their and everyone else's day. Within the newborn nursery, differences in temperament among infants can be clearly observed almost immediately. Although we may be born a certain way, the wonder of human beings is our capacity to consciously and willfully make choices. Ultimately, it is the choices we either make or don't make that make us what we are. Whether a person is born unhappy or learns to feel unfulfilled as a result of life's injuries, it is of little solace to classroom teachers when they dump their anger on us. I suppose the best that can be said is to try to roll with the punches, side step the jabs and refuse to take the anger personally. Try to realize that the child of an unhappy parent is likely to need more compassion and nurturing so when you get angry at the child, remember what he has to experience regularly at home. Try also to realize that many difficult parents were themselves poorly parented and carry unresolved resentment to those in authority.

The main goal with these parents is to try to defuse

their anger as much as possible. At the same time, do not back down on policies and procedures that are educationally sound but may be targeted by them as a bulls-eye for their anger. These parents will endlessly complain about something, so it can be a challenge to not throw out the baby with the bathwater. Try to hear their concerns without being stung by their delivery.

THE BIG PICTURE

There are five attitudes, beliefs and understandings that are at the core of all the strategies that are offered in this book. Embracing these attitudes can make it much easier to work effectively with difficult parents. Some difficult parents are misguided advocates who mean well but just go about it in the wrong way. They care about their kids and want to stick up for them but they do it in a way that alienates rather than collaborates. If we can look beyond their anger and see them as having something to teach us, we are apt to be far less defensive when they are disagreeable. Further, we may well learn something helpful about their child. Sometimes, we may just need to come to grips with the reality that some parents are unhappy people whose own negative school or life experience continually colors their interactions with others. Although we may need to ultimately set limits when they cross our line, we need to find it within our hearts to extend caring and empathy even when they show us blame and anger. At all times our actions need to be guided by what we believe is educationally sound, yet we must always strive to express this with proper respect and dignity even when others seem undeserving. More on each of these attitudes follows on the next page.

1. VIEW DIFFICULT PARENTS AS MISGUIDED ADVOCATES

Try hard to realize that an angry parent is better than an absent parent! While angry parents can be very unpleasant, their anger conveys advocacy. As much as you might disagree with a parent's complaint, the fact that the parent is sharing it shows that she cares about her child. When we view complaints, anger and threats as misguided advocacy, it makes it possible for us to continue working with the parent because the only issue becomes our disagreement with *what* is being advocated. Virtually all parents, including most who border on acting irrationally, will cooperate if they really believe that you care about their child, are eager to help their child achieve success and are helping their child become more responsible.

2. VIEW DIFFICULT PARENTS AS HAVING SOMETHING TO TEACH

If everybody cooperated, there would probably be little to learn. When pushed by difficult students and/or their parents, we can either try to avoid them, fight back or learn from them. Realistically, we won't be able to avoid them. Some will be omnipresent and very quick to complain about perceived wrongdoing. Fighting with them usually leads to more stress and conflict. A wise teacher I know once told a student that he was convinced God put the boy in his class to make him a better teacher. Since he had not yet figured out how to motivate interest in this child, the wise teacher reasoned that he still had something to learn, and this was God's way of telling him. As Henry Ford once said, "failure is the opportunity to begin again a little more intelligently." It is a strange thing that when people feel appreciated, even if for no other reason than they are challenging to get along with, their cooperation improves. Ask yourself what there might be to learn from a difficult parent. Try to allow yourself to get beyond your raw emotions and see things from the parent's perspective.

I remember Mrs. Skinner, whose presence and complaints made teachers of Danny, her physically disabled and learning impaired son, roll their eyes upon seeing her. She was ornery, sarcastic and caustic. She always seemed to focus on the negative despite many fine efforts being made to accommodate her son by school professionals. In short, a visit from Mrs. Skinner was to say the least, an unpleasant event. In actuality, her frustration was often palpable as she struggled to get a supportive but rigid school system to address her child's needs. I came to respect Mrs. Skinner for her unyielding devotion to Danny. Once I got past her abrasive manner, I was able to learn a lot about Danny from listening to her. We were then able to develop many different learning strategies that not only helped Danny, but were also helpful to other students. Years later, I still receive much caring and warmth from her.

3. BE GUIDED BY WHAT IS EDUCATIONALLY SOUND, NOT POLITICALLY CORRECT

Be guided by what you believe is in the best educational interests of your students. Teachers are on solid footing when we are guided by two primary goals: *doing everything in our power to help students be successful* and *furthering the development of responsible student behavior.* In addition, we need to reinforce the values most parents want their children to learn. In some cases, we must be prepared to teach the values that parents should want their children to learn: responsibility, tolerance, safety and the ability to effectively communicate with others.

In this era, too many educators are easily intimidated, believing they will receive little administrative support if parents complain. While it is true that few educators look forward to battling difficult parents, do not allow your actions to be guided by fear. Do what is educationally sound, not what is politically correct! When you are managing a tough situation, be guided by what you can do to help your students be successful and/or what kind of actions or consequences are likely to teach them more about responsibility. Actions guided by these two goals will always be respected if not applauded. Although not all conflict between a teacher and administrator generated by a complaining parent can be

avoided, much of it can. Teachers need to be ready to explain the purpose of actions they take in terms of how these actions are designed to teach the student responsibility or help the student achieve academic success. Administrators need to consult teachers about intended actions before these actions are put into effect. Perhaps of greatest importance for educators is that we give all of our students what we believe they need without worrying about treating each one the same way. When parents complain about unfair treatment that their child has received, we must be prepared to learn from the parent without backing away from the two fundamental goals: *__success__* and *__responsibility__*. As Thomas Jefferson said long ago, "there is nothing so unequal as treating unequals equally."

4. CONVEY RESPECT & DIGNITY

It is easy for well-mannered educators to act with respect and dignity when all is going well. The challenge is to convey these attitudes when anger, disagreement, and finger pointing are coming your way. In all of your interactions with parents, respond towards them in ways you want them to respond to you. Model what you expect. When needing to give feedback to a parent and you are unsure what to say, try putting yourself at the receiving end. How would you want

to be spoken to by someone else who is about to give you feedback about your child? If a parent gets mad and starts using language that you find offensive, act in a way that is consistent with what you are trying to teach your students. What would you want your students to say or do if they were being verbally assaulted? How would you want them to re-act? If parents express anger, work to defuse them in a manner similar to how you would want your students to defuse each other. When your line has been crossed, set limits firmly yet respectfully.

5. BE QUICK TO FORGIVE AND DIFFICULT TO OFFEND

When working to get the best out of people, it is fine to hold them accountable for what they do, but be quick in your heart to forgive their transgressions. Don't clutter your hard drive with the "spam" of anger and resentment when others say or do hurtful things. Listen, respond and be as-sertive when necessary, but be sure to hit your emo-tional "delete" button early and often when others say or do things that push your buttons.

Deleted that Spam!

20

USING THE BOOK MOST EFFECTIVELY

This is a book of practical strategies that are designed to prevent problems before they occur and to offer effective interventions when necessary. The strategies are grouped into four categories for ease of reference. *Strategies that set the right tone* provide numerous ideas about what to do within the first month of school in order to get parents on your side. These strategies are designed to build positive relationships and develop trust early in the school year although it is never too late to benefit from them. In essence these are ways of connecting with all parents by being welcoming, including those who are most difficult. *Strategies to gain and keep parental support throughout the school year* offer many practical ways of keeping things positive between school and home. These are easy to implement relationship methods that keep teachers and parents working collaboratively on behalf of the student. *Strategies that provide advice and support* are designed to be highly practical suggestions that educators can offer parents to help them motivate their children to learn and interact with their children in ways that are likely to yield cooperation and responsible be-

havior. Some of these tips and suggestions offer frustrated parents support and information to help parents handle challenging situations with their children. ***Successfully handling difficult moments*** provides effective ways of dealing with aggressive and uncooperative parents when they accuse or make unreasonable demands. In this section, ways of effectively setting limits with unreasonable parents are presented, as are specific methods for defusing volatile parents. Each section offers strategies, tips and ideas about how to gain cooperation and support from colleagues and administrators when necessary.

STRATEGIES THAT SET THE RIGHT TONE WITH DIFFICULT PARENTS

The strategies in this section can be useful at all times but are particularly effective when begun within the first month of school. Some of these strategies are designed to develop a positive relationship with difficult-to-reach parents by identifying effective ways of establishing communication with them. Other strategies show specific things to say and do that demonstrate interest in their child so that common ground is found with difficult parents. Finally, some strategies show how to establish and communicate effective rules and consequences to parents based upon school values that are necessary to promote success and further responsibility.

GET ON THEIR SIDE EARLY – It is often little things that will get parents to want to cooperate. Spend some time early in the school year figuring out who your challenging students are likely to be, and make contact with their parents. Demonstrate interest by introducing yourself either in person or by phone. Tell them that you expect all

of your students to be successful in your class, identify a few important guidelines that you expect your students to follow that will help them be successful and ask what they believe you can do to be a great teacher for their child. Quite simply, you want to show that you care by enthusiastically expressing your desire to make it a successful year for their child. Parents give us a lot of rope when they believe that we care about their child. Reported in the bestseller *BLINK (2005),* is a study conducted by Wendy Levinson. Hundreds of conversations between physicians and their patients were recorded. Roughly half had been sued for malpractice at least twice with the other half never having been sued. Levinson (1997) found that there was no difference in the medical mistakes between those who had been sued and those who had not. Physicians who had never been sued spent twenty percent more time with their patients and showed more personal interest by engaging in active listening. The bottom line is patients don't sue doctors they like who show they care. If physicians can avoid malpractice lawsuits by spending a few more caring minutes with a patient, is it unreasonable to assume that teachers can avoid a lot of bellyaching from parents by conveying the human touch?

MAKE AT LEAST TWO PHONE CALLS HOME BEFORE THERE ARE PROBLEMS – Your first phone call to a parent should ideally be to introduce yourself and your program. It is best done before school begins and it is a general phone call during which you tell parents that you are looking forward to having their child in your class this year. Let them know how important it is to you that their child succeeds. You might give a brief overview of content but it is most important to emphasize the importance of study skills and keeping organized. Be clear and specific in letting them know what factors are most important for success in your classroom. Let them know you consider failure to be an unacceptable option. You might ask them to describe their child in terms of study habits and organizational skills. As well, ask them to tell you a little bit about their child's past school experience, how she best learns and what interests she has *(see figure 1)*. The second phone call should be made sometime during the first two weeks. Offer a genuine compliment about something the student accomplished either academically or behaviorally.

FIND OUT THE BEST WAY(S) OF COMMUNICATING WITH THEM – During an early in the school year phone call or at your first visit during an event such as open house, try

to ascertain the best way(s) for you to communicate with parents. Give them information such as your e-mail address and school phone number, and let them know the best times(s) you can be reached. Tell them that parent involvement is crucial to student success, and invite them to tell you how they can be reached. Suggest that they provide their e-mail address so that you can send them occasional updates. Incidentally, some teachers have found it extremely beneficial to give parents their home phone number while letting them know that while they prefer being reached at school, parents should not hesitate to call when they have something important to express. You can make this palatable by identifying a specific time that works for you and letting students and parents know (i.e. "Mr. Jones' 7:00-7:30 Evening Half-hour"). Most teachers find that few if any parents call them at home, so there is actually very little inconvenience. The benefit is that most parents will feel very confident knowing the teacher cares that much.

HAVE PARENT(S) FILL OUT AN INTEREST INVENTORY ABOUT THEIR CHILD – Ask all of your students' parents to complete an interest inventory about their child so that you can learn about interests, strengths and needs from

FIGURE 1

INTEREST INVENTORY

Dear Parent:

Please take a moment to fill out this interest inventory. I am eager to do whatever I can to make your child's school experience successful, meaningful and pleasant. I appreciate the opportunity to gain from your knowledge of your child. Thank you.

My child's name is_____.

Something my child likes to do outside of school is_____.

My child's favorite time of year is_____.

For my child, school is_____.

When my child gets older, I hope _____.

During my child's free time, he/she prefers _____.

A place my child likes to visit is_____.

My child's favorite hobby is_____.

My child's favorite subject in school is_____.

My child's least favorite subject in school is_____.

With other people my child_____.

When my child does not get his/her way at home_____.

When my child is alone_____.

When my child misbehaves it works best to_____.

The best way to communicate with me _____.

Important things to know about my child's life outside of school that might affect his/her achievement in the classroom are_____.

Parent or Guardian(s) Name_____

the perspective of the parent(s). Be sure to include opportunities for parents to express their preferences about what they believe is best to do to promote their child's strengths as well as how to handle problems should they occur.

SOLICIT A BRIEF INFORMATION SURVEY FROM PARENTS – If the interest inventory is a bit too much for you, in a note, letter or during open house, let parents know you will try to meet each student's needs. In order to be successful, let parents know that you would like their help. Ask them for:

   a. Three things that your child likes to do.

   b. Three things that your child has liked best about school.

   c. What are two or three things you have noticed that best help your child learn?

   d. What are some things that I should know that could help me make school a successful place for your child?

IDENTIFY KEY VALUES THAT ARE REQUIRED FOR SUCCESS: SAFETY, RESPECT, PERSEVERANCE – We are on safe ground when we promote the values we know we need to have in order for good teaching and learning to occur.

Convey to parents that school is the equivalent of a child's place of work. Just as there are certain behaviors expected at work, so too there are appropriate ways of behaving at school. If parents claim that their child has a right to defend himself by fighting, point out that fighting would not be tolerated in the workplace for any reason, and in fact the worker might well lose his job. Educators cannot be in the business of firing students! The stakes are too high. Instead, we must be prepared to teach and show proper ways of handling situations that will not get them into trouble. People only get better at things when they practice the skill, not when they are excluded from the opportunity. Respectfully acknowledge your appreciation for the frustration that a parent might be feeling in encouraging a student to behave in an unacceptable way, while clearly expressing to the parent an acceptable alternative. For example:

At school, when students are unhappy with each other, we encourage them to tell how they feel and what they want. If Steve didn't like what Stu said to him, then we teach that he can either walk away or say, "Steve, I don't appreciate when you talk to me like that."

Conclude with,

"I am glad we are having this conversation, because it would be so helpful for you to encourage this message at

29

home as well. How can I help you do that?"

CONNECT CLASSROOM RULES TO THESE VALUES –

In many previous publications, I have advocated the importance of involving students in developing and even assisting with the enforcement of classroom rules. Students experience ownership when they have a voice in developing rules and as a result are more apt to follow them. Yet more important than rules are the values that give rules their foundation and meaning. While rules are designed to tell students what to do or how to do it, the goal of a value is defining why the specific rules are needed. Without values, rules can feel arbitrary. With values, rules make sense. For example, a speed limit sign tells a driver how fast he may go (the rule), but is most likely to be followed in the absence of a police officer when it makes sense (the value). We are more apt to follow a speed limit sign to slow down on a residential street in the middle of the day to the sight and sound of children playing than we are at midnight on that same street. Be sure that the classroom rules connect to the values you are promoting. For example, TAKE CARE OF YOURSELF; TAKE CARE OF EACH OTHER; TAKE CARE OF THIS PLACE are values that encourage safety, respect and perseverance.

Rules and procedures should be based on these values with input encouraged by your students. It is wise to inform parents of the values that will be the foundation of the classroom rules and consequences. You can invite their input about rules or procedures that they believe will best help their child behave according to these values.

SEEK ADMINISTRATIVE SUPPORT BY HAVING VALUES AND RULES ENDORSED BY THEM – After identifying your classroom values and rules, seek administrative support. Explain why these values are necessary for good teaching and learning to occur, and how the rules support the values. Make sure that you are guided by what you believe is best for the <u>students.</u> This is also a good time to let your administrator know that should there ever be a concern expressed by a parent to the administrator about something you did, you would greatly appreciate being consulted before any decisions are made. It is entirely appropriate to ask that the administrator redirect the parent before becoming strongly involved in the matter. It may be necessary to emphasize this point since administrators can be put under considerable pressure by some parents to take action immediately.

EXPLAIN THAT YOU WILL BE FAIR AND THAT YOU MAY NOT ALWAYS TREAT ALL STUDENTS THE SAME –

Early in the school year during open house, explain that promoting *success* and *responsibility* are your two primary goals. Let parents know that you will do whatever it takes to assist their child to become as successful as possible and to learn as much as she can about being a responsible learner in school. Since not all students learn the same way or at the same pace, you will often adjust assignments to promote success and provide different consequences when necessary if students break rules. If one student can do three math problems but another can do ten, then there will be different math assignments based upon helping each become better at math. If two students break a rule, you will do whatever is necessary to help each student learn not to make the same mistake again. Let parents know that you welcome whatever ideas and suggestions they may have to help their child become more successful or responsible in your class. If parents complain about what you are doing with their child, acknowledge their complaint but explain your actions in terms of success and responsibility (i.e. "If I understand correctly, you disagree with the consequence I gave Mary. Since I really value your support, I gave her that conse-

quence because it is my belief that it will help her not make the same mistake again. However, I am open to other alternatives that might work just as well. Are there any ideas you have that I might have missed?")

HAVE A PREDICTABLE TIME TO BE AVAILABLE – As a teacher, you are entitled to a life away from your students and their parents. You can limit your availability and keep yourself accessible by having predictable times to meet, answer calls and return e-mails. In this era of instant information, most people expect an immediate response to their inquiry or comment. Be sure to state when you will be returning calls and e-mails. For example,

"If you have questions about your child, I welcome your phone calls and e-mails. All phone calls and e-mails received prior to 2 p.m. will be returned the same day unless some rare special circumstance keeps me from doing so. Phone calls and e-mails received after 2 p.m. will be returned as soon as possible the next day."

HAVE A FAMILY CLASS PICNIC – This is a nice touch to do at a strategic time such as the beginning of school, before a new semester begins, or to celebrate the coming of Spring. Make personal contact through e-mail, phone or

letter to invite your more difficult parents.

BE GUIDED BY TLC – It is an old but true cliché that all children need tender, loving, care. The TLC acronym has been appropriately redefined by Kindlon (2003) to mean TIME, LIMITS, CARING. Our role as educators can be similarly defined. Are we emphasizing these traits at least as strongly as our curriculum? Teachers generally get more motivated and better-behaved students when they do. While it is beyond our role to proselytize to parents, offer them your knowledge of this acronym so that they can be well guided. Jesse Jackson once said, "Your children need your presence more than your presents."

EMPHASIZE EDUCATING THE STUDENT RATHER THAN FAMILY OR CULTURE – We must be certain to ensure that what we do provides the individual student with the best chance of success even if parents disagree. Although we can be sensitive to family history, personal and cultural values, when these get in the way of providing a student with opportunities for success, we must be brave enough to stand up for what we believe. I was recently asked in an interview how to handle a situation where certain Hispanic parents only valued education for their son and

not their daughter. My answer was and is that it is not our role as an educator to predetermine an outcome for a student. It is our job to educate individuals, not families or cultures. If this educated daughter has to deal with family conflict because she is following her dream that is being encouraged by her teacher, then that is a problem she will have to deal with as an individual. When we educators are overly sensitive to a family's wish for their child or a perceived cultural norm, we run the risk of discriminating against the individual's hopes and dreams.

If parents have goals for their children that may run counter to educational excellence, it is wise to involve your counselor or administrator.

STRATEGIES TO GAIN AND KEEP PARENTAL SUPPORT THROUGHOUT THE SCHOOL YEAR

The strategies in this section have two goals. Some are designed to show ways of preventing problems from developing with difficult parents. These are simple, easy to implement strategies to make and keep your classroom a welcoming place. Other strategies show how to keep problems with difficult parents from dominating your time and energy.

SEND COMPLIMENTARY NOTES HOME OCCASIONALLY –

Sending a note to parents about an achievement or accomplishment pertaining to their child often generates much support from them. Everyone likes to hear good news and will be much more receptive to cooperating when their help is needed. Make an effort at least twice a year to do this for each child. Students or parents who are more challenging should be written to more often. It can occasionally be very powerful to write a "paradoxical" note to a parent after a student who has been showing improvement behaves poorly. Then give the note to the student and ask him to give it to his mother. For example, after Joey has had a difficult day, his teacher writes,

Dear Mrs. Lankovich,
I just want to tell you what a pleasure it is to have Joey in my class. He has been really making an effort to pay more attention and get his work done. Please tell him how pleased you are and remind him to keep up the good work.

Many teachers are reluctant to do this for fear of reinforcing bad behavior. Although this is an understandable concern, keep in mind that behavior change is a roller coaster ride. The student will hear the more powerful message of teacher appreciation for behavioral improvement. Most students are entirely able to contrast the appreciation given by the teacher with the poor behavior that they know is inappropriate and unacceptable. Improved behavior usually follows because the student has been powerfully and privately thanked while being reminded that he is entirely capable of offering better behavior.

CALL AND LEAVE A POSITIVE MESSAGE ON THE ANSWER MACHINE – Virtually everyone's phone has the capacity to record a message when they are not home. This is great for teachers because it enables us to leave positive messages quickly while saving us the time of actually having a conversation with a parent. Simply call when you think nobody will be home and share your appreciation about something positive done or accomplished by the student. This can be especially useful after you have discussed a concern you have with a parent and notice improvement in the child. End with something like,

"Thanks for your help at influencing Sally because improvement is definitely happening. If you want to call back feel free, but there really is no need. Just wanted to let you know."

Needless to say, if somebody actually answers, don't hang up!!

SMILE AND BE FRIENDLY – The saying "attitude is everything" applies mightily to the degree of success we can experience as teachers. Although there are many factors that affect our students over which we have little if any control, we are in charge of the attitude that we bring to school every day. Strive to make your classroom become a retreat, an island or sanctuary of safety, support and connectedness to which students (and parents) look forward to coming. See yourself as a merchant seeking customers. You need a good product, presented in an attractive way that is affordable to your customers. The good product is the material to be presented.

Think of a store or place that you love to go. What characteristics of the people or environment make you want to go there? Try to simulate these characteristics in your classroom in order to provide the equivalent of an attractive, affordable place. Probably you find your favorite place(s) includes friendly people who make you feel welcome. See your students and their parents as your customers. The world famous FISH market in Seattle encourages its employees to "choose your attitude," and "make their (customers) day."

MAKE SCHOOL BELONG TO PARENTS – Gaining cooperation from difficult parents becomes much easier when parents feel truly welcome. Too often, we make parents feel like outsiders, welcoming them only during an open school night in which they get to meet us in a very unreal way. School signs should be friendly. Instead of "All visitors must report to the office," signs ought to state,

If you are a parent, thank you for coming today. We are thrilled that you are at school. For safety reasons, please stop by the office, say hello and sign in. Please help yourself to a donut and some coffee.

Parents who feel welcome are much more likely to volunteer or attend after-school events. They can be made to feel important by being given important things to do. Feeling purposeful is a powerful motivator. Seek volunteers from the school's main language groups to telephone hard-to-reach parents and have them serve as translators for conferencing when necessary. Ask parents to record children's books or textbook material for the school's books-on-tape library. Give rubrics to parents so they know what to look for in their child's work.

STRATEGIES

Make Parents feel welcome.

Choose your attitude.

Seek their feedback.

Invite Parents to share interests.

Offer hope.

Invite challenging parents or parents of challenging students to advocate for change appropriately through a site-based school council or committee that is seeking to improve some aspect(s) of school life. Difficult parents will sometimes offer effective ideas. Even when they don't, this kind of involvement provides a forum in which they can share their ideas and learn from others in a more comfortable, non-adversarial environment. Most parents like talking about their own children and when they are given an opportunity, they will often share how their child spends time at home or why their child might be experiencing school problems. In this type of setting, it can be easier to make challenged and challenging parents aware of social services and community agencies. Follow-up can be done later in a more personalized way by directing the parent to the resource(s) that is most appropriate.

TELL PARENTS ABOUT SCHOOL ASSIGNMENTS (PROJECTS) THAT WILL INVOLVE THEIR TIME – In the quest to differentiate instruction and address students with different learning styles, the requirement for "hands-on" projects has become quite common. Too often, students bring assignments home that require much parental direction and support for successful completion. It is common for parents to have to shop for materials with their children, explain specifics and provide organizational support.

Although it is reasonable to expect some academic help from home, there are some students in each school whose parents are physically, intellectually or emotionally unavailable to provide the level of support needed for success. In some cases, there is simply too much of this requirement hoisted upon parents. In my mind, a school assignment should be the responsibility of students and it should fully be the teacher's responsibility to provide whatever materials and organizational support without expecting academic help to come from home. At most, information should be given about the project including its purpose and materials that children will be provided. If a project will require direct involvement from the parent, this should be stated in advance along with a solid rationale.

Students should not be punished for parents who cannot or will not provide the type of support that might be needed. And parents should be unashamedly invited to let the teacher know when projects create undue stress for the child or themselves so that other arrangements can be made.

HAVE A SUGGESTION BOX – Welcome input from your students and their parents by having a suggestion box. Encourage them to offer feedback that might improve the class. For example, be open to having fun as long as learning occurs. Be open to any and all suggestions a parent has that she believes will lead to greater success and growth in responsibility. Invite suggestions on your or the school's web site. Let all know that you read the suggestions daily, and if signed, you will either follow the suggestion or contact the writer for more discussion.

HAVE A PLACE FOR PARENTS – Schools that want to engage parents in positive ways set aside comfortable space to include them. Certainly, it is wise for all teachers to genuinely invite parents to come into the class to observe and participate. In addition, a good school-wide process is to have a "parent" room set up with comfortable furniture, books and videos that parents might find interesting, along with available food and coffee. It is best if someone is there to welcome them, perhaps a staff member on a rotating basis or a representative from PTO. This can also be effective with "hovering" parents who are forever present. Having a "parent space" can provide a place to redirect parents who for whatever reason need to constantly be at school. When there is a predetermined space that belongs to parents, it is often easier to set limits around classroom visits, which can be a welcome development in containing the potentially harmful influence of hovering parents whose constant presence can interfere with their child's healthy development.

MAKE A HOME OR CHURCH VISIT– Many teachers lament how few parents come to school for events that may be considered important. While it is indeed frustrating when few parents attend a special program designed for them or a parent-teacher conference, we need to be flexible in finding ways of reaching out to them on turf that is more comfortable. Remember that some parents are preoccupied with the very basic needs of life and struggling to survive while others may avoid school because of negative feelings they have developed based upon either their child's experience or their own.

Make an occasional home visit either as a way of introducing yourself or when you need to share important information and suspect that the parent will have difficulty coming to school. If you fear going to the neighborhood, travel with a partner. Perhaps you can ask an administrator to join you. Not only will most parents appreciate your effort, your administrator will also get to see the depth of your commitment to your students.

When you want to get word out about a school program that might interest or require parent involvement, consider contacting the local church pastor for guidance. Although separation of church and state is the law of the land, educators too often underutilize the church connection to inform and perhaps influence. Connect with the community's religious leaders when you want to provide a program of importance to parents. Explain the purpose and probable benefits. If you can sell them on the idea, then ask them to help you get the word out to parents. You might ask for their opinion as to the best ways of informing their congregants. In a similar vein, if you learn that a disconnected school parent is more closely connected at church, you might try contacting the minister for advice as to how to best reach this parent.

DO COMMUNITY OUTREACH WITH STUDENTS AND INVITE SPECIFIC PARENTS TO BE CHAPERONES – Many high schools require community service as a condition for graduation. Long before graduation, involve your challenging parents in these efforts. One of the best ways to build cooperation is by working together towards a common purpose that is valued by all. Difficult parents can become excellent

partners in the planning and execution of such initiatives. It gives them a chance to share special moments with their child and with you. I recently had an opportunity to share an outreach experience working in a soup kitchen with my daughter, some of her classmates, their parents and her teacher. I felt a special closeness with her and all of the others as we worked for a common good. As the parent of an adolescent, it can be particularly difficult to find special moments to share. Good feelings develop when the school becomes a place where parents, students and teachers can share meaningful moments.

Although time-consuming and perhaps not always possible when instruction is paramount, these kinds of initiatives can get started by innovative teachers with the bulk of the planning and work done outside class. For example, a reading of *Lord of the Rings* might lead to discussion about how people working together for a positive common purpose can avoid the formation and influence of harmful peer groups. Brainstorming community projects that could provide real benefits while simultaneously getting students and perhaps their parents to organize as the "doers" may follow. Students can then be encouraged to step forward as leaders of groups that will flesh out ideas and relevant projects. Being the leaders, students invite parents to join at various junctures based upon the project and its plan. Periodically, the teacher can monitor how things are going.

SEND HOME A PHOTO OF A CHILD ENGAGED IN A SCHOOL ACTIVITY – Most parents love to see pictures of their children engaged in meaningful, fun activities. Even better are photographs of the child at school being in charge of something important that is valued in the classroom. If you have a digital camera, shoot photos of your students involved in a wide variety of activities that you can later review and either e-mail these to the student's family or print a hard copy. When there is a problem with the child separating from a parent, a variation of this idea can be very helpful. Ask the parent to provide you with one or more family photographs that you can give to the child when she is "missing" her parent(s). This can help alleviate the child's anxiety and perhaps that of the parent as well.

SEND A HOLIDAY CARD TO THE FAMILY AND A BIRTH-DAY CARD TO YOUR STUDENTS – During the holiday season, send a card to the family along with a short personal greeting.

Something simple such as:

"To the Crawford family: Enjoy the holiday.
Jamal, I look forward to seeing you after break."

A birthday card from the teacher with a personalized statement, is awesomely appreciated by students and recognized by parents.

USE E-MAIL TO COMMUNICATE – This used to be a novel idea but now most schools have websites and teachers can easily be reached through a link. Use your e-mail to keep parents and students informed about upcoming events and classroom happenings. You can also easily post assignments along with due dates. With difficult parents, make a point of communicating with them about something at least once a week through e-mail. You can also use this conduit to share good news. If you haven't heard from a challenging parent for awhile, initiate contact and ask for feedback. Probably things have been going relatively well which is why you haven't been hearing from them. It is a good time to enhance your relationship with them so that when you need their support, they are more likely to be there.

CALL PARENTS AT WORK TO SHARE GOOD NEWS –

When good things happen, call parents at work at least once. Although this may initially be greeted with trepidation and concern since most parents worry about bad news when they receive a call from school, pride and joy will quickly be experienced. If someone else at work answers, ask to speak to the student's parent while identifying yourself as a school person who wants to share some really good news about something that just happened at school.

When parents hear good things and they are at work, not only will they feel pleased, they are also likely to share their good fortune with everyone around them. Most co-workers (who also likely have children at school) will view you and your school in a very positive way. A sample dialogue might go something like this:

"Hello Mr. Jones. This is Mrs. Heniger, Brian's teacher at school. I am sure you are busy and I don't want to take too much of your time. Rarely do I call parents at work because I know how inconvenient that can be, but while I had a minute I just wanted to let you know how good I feel about Brian's work and behavior. He has really been making an effort to do his best and I am feeling very proud of him. I just wanted to let you know. Have a great day."

REFRAME THE STUDENT – Is the glass half full or half empty? How we see things can influence what we get. The frame we put around a photograph can be as important to the overall impression as the picture itself. Is a difficult student oppositional or persistent, stubborn or determined, defiant or tenacious, wiggly or energetic, lazy or laid back? If we can view a problem as a strength, the better able we can be at exerting influence because we start at a place where students and their parents feel appreciated. Most parents know the challenges presented by tough kids, but they really appreciate adults who show a willingness to engage and build the strengths their children have.

Students and parents most resist change when they feel forced to let go of the familiar. Cooperation from challenging parents is best sought when we view the problems caused by their children as opportunities to build on their strengths. For example, the teacher who is able to view the normally <u>defiant</u> Billy as <u>determined</u> has more ability to positively influence change in his behavior. For example, she can intervene with,

"Billy, you are one of the strongest, most determined students in this class. In fact, I have yet to find a consequence that gets you to turn in your work. And even though it makes my job harder, I think it can be a sign

of much strength when a person stands up for himself. Maybe you can help me solve my problem. You see, when you don't do your work, it makes it really hard to know if I am being a good teacher for you, and that bothers me. It is important that I am a good teacher for you. So even though I can't make you do the assignment today, I hope you do it anyway so that I can know that you are learning. By the way, I can live with you doing either the first three problems or the last three. If you want to do all six, okay. But I can live with you making the choice. Which can I look forward to seeing by the end of class?"

As the student becomes less resistant and more successful in your class, his parent(s) are more likely to feel good about him and the school. The whole cycle of change becomes reinforced.

WHEN GIVING FEEDBACK START WITH THE POSITIVE –

Many parents of difficult students can be very defensive with some becoming quite protective of their child. Even when you are meeting to discuss concerns and issues that need improvement, start with strengths. You might begin by welcoming the parent. For example, "Thank you Mrs. Jones for coming in so that we can figure out how

to help Leticia be more successful." Next is to brainstorm strengths with the parent, "I'd like to start by asking you to tell me about her strengths and I would like to share some things that I notice as well." It can be powerful to actually write these strengths down on the chalkboard or on a large sheet of newsprint as you and the parent brainstorm. Doing this identifies you as a partner with the parent and sets the stage for more successful problem-solving later. In addition, you can learn a lot about your student and maybe even build upon the strengths identified at home.

Jim's Strengths

- Always is smiling
- Stands up for himself
- Has a mind of his own
- Works hard when interested
- Can be helpful towards others

CALL OR ASK FOR OCCASIONAL FEEDBACK – It is a good idea to seek parental input before you hear about problems. Be open to knowing how you are doing from the perspective of the parent. There may be parents that are harboring resentment about things that you are doing (or that they think you are doing), which may not be difficult to change. You might send a feedback survey a few times each year to either all or some of your parents so that you can stay informed. The following can be included:

As a parent, you are so very important to your child's success at school. I am eager to know how you view your child's experience in my class. Please take a few moments to answer the following questions, since your feedback can be very helpful in making sure that your child is getting the best possible experience he/she can.

1. *How do you think your child is doing in my class?*

2. **How do you think your child should be doing in my class?**

3. *What do you hear your child talking about that he/she likes?*

4. **Is there anything that can be improved that would make your child more successful (Please be specific)?**

5. *Would you like to discuss any concerns you may have?*

6. **What is the best way and time to contact you?**

DEVELOP A METHOD OF FEEDBACK THAT WORKS FOR YOU AND PARENTS (i.e. DAILY NOTE HOME) –

When you have a sense that a parent is rarely satisfied and often questions your actions, develop a method of regular feedback that works for both of you. This can be in the form of written daily feedback in a student's notebook, a weekly phone call home, a chart that you send home on a regular basis that lets the parent know how the child is doing *(see figure 2)*, or some other mutually acceptable form of feedback. The feedback should be cooperative in that parents are encouraged to respond to the specifics you offer with an opportunity to contact you to share their impressions. The feedback can also include a way for the parent to initiate comments or suggestions should she wish.

ASK THE OPINION OF A DIFFICULT PARENT –

Parents who are chronically difficult usually have a frustrated need for power and influence. In actuality, most feel that nobody listens or really cares what they think. In fact, it is not unusual for them to believe (sometimes correctly) that they have lost much of their influence with their own children. As mentioned earlier, getting angry and blaming the school can be a way for them to form an alliance with their chil-

FIGURE 2

SUCCESS FOR JOHNNY

PUT FORTH EFFORT　　　　　　　Excellent　5　4　3　2　1　Poor
Comments:

Your (parent) feedback or ideas to help me understand:

DID HIS WORK WITH GOOD QUALITY Excellent　5　4　3　2　1　Poor
Comments:

Your feedback or ideas to help me understand:

GOT ALONG WITH OTHERS　　　　Excellent　5　4　3　2　1　Poor
Comments:

Your feedback or ideas to help me understand:

FOLLOWED THE RULES　　　　　　Excellent　5　4　3　2　1　Poor
Comments:

Your feedback or ideas to help me understand

HANDLED HIS EMOTIONS　　　　　Excellent　5　4　3　2　1　Poor
Comments:

dren against a common "enemy." It can be very effective
to seek opinions from these parents before they complain.
Invite them to come to school meetings when you know
policy issues will be discussed so they can have input. When
seeking parental input about classroom rules or procedures,
parents who complain can actually be quite helpful. The

idea is to give them a voice BEFORE they complain so they feel heard and respected. Opinions about how their child might react to something you are planning can be solicited as well. For example, after the usual greetings, you might say to a difficult parent, "Here is what I am planning to do. I am wondering what you think," or "My goal is for each student in the class to learn more about responsibility at the playground. Do you have any ideas that you think could be good for your child and perhaps other children as well?"

INVITE DIFFICULT PARENTS TO SPEND TIME OBSERVING YOUR CLASS – As unpleasant as the thought might be to have a difficult parent observe, this can be a powerful tool towards inviting cooperation. It is particularly effective when parents are blaming you based upon what they heard from their child. When a child has been in trouble, it is common for them to tell their side of the story to their parent(s). Naturally, no child will ever say, *"Mrs. Jones got mad today because I was throwing flying missiles in the classroom, tapping my pencil endlessly and I constantly got out of my seat to bother other students while smirking at her as she was trying to correct me."* Instead, most kids portray the teacher as having been unfair, needlessly picking on them. When this happens regu-

larly, invite parents to visit your class and then listen to strategies they might offer that can best help their child. Should they show no interest, offer the option of videotaping so that you and they can review the behavior of their child at some future time. Needless to say, it is best to initiate contact when problems are in their early stage and long before they have gained a major foothold.

INVITE DIFFICULT PARENTS TO SHARE AN INTEREST OF THEIRS – One of the best ways to get parents positively involved in your classroom is to have them share their interests and talents with your students. It is relatively easy to ascertain interests from parents who are already heavily involved in their child's learning. At an elementary level, you can simply tell parents that you would like your students to learn as much about the world as they can. Express your enthusiasm in having parents share an aspect of their job or hobby that they find exciting. Then invite them to share this with your students. You might have to do a little more "fishing" to get difficult parents involved. Try to find out what their interests are. Ask parents to volunteer a half-hour to share and demonstrate what they do. Even during a meeting in which they are complaining to you about something, try to redirect the conversation in a way that gets them to share their strengths. For example,

"Gee Mrs. Huang, I totally understand your concerns and I think you have some really great ideas. I'm glad we had a chance to meet. You know, I understand from Bobby that you like knitting and I was wondering if you might come to class and show the children what you do. I think this might be an especially worthwhile activity for some of my students who need a little more "hands-on." When are you available?"

EMPHASIZE YOUR DESIRE TO PROMOTE SUCCESS IN THEIR CHILD – Keep your focus on promoting success. Let the parent know what is expected for success to occur. Show flexibility in doing whatever it takes to help their child be successful but connect every suggestion parents have to this outcome. If they want you to do something that flies in the face of success, be honest. Tell them,

"Much as I would like to agree with you, I just can't do what you are asking. If I did what you are asking, I am afraid that I would be expecting less from your child than I know he is capable of achieving. Help me figure out what we can do that will help us all feel better and also help Bobby get his work done at a level we all

know he is capable of achieving."

Parents respect teachers who have realistically high expectations of their child.

OFFER STUDENTS WRITTEN FEEDBACK THAT INSPIRES

HOPE – The best way to avoid unnecessary conflict with parents is to have satisfied students. Students tend to be most motivated and best behaved when the classroom is a relevant place, provides adequate depth and continually provides students with confidence and belief in their ability to be successful. Naturally, honest feedback that points to improvement is essential as well, but even corrective feedback is best received on a foundation of hope. The following responses are examples of written feedback (you can give these orally as well) that tend to inspire hope in students:

"Thanks for all the thought you put into this assignment."

"It looks like you really put forth some effort in this."

"I am especially impressed by these ideas (specify)."

"I like how you_____. It would be nice to read more from you about_____."

"Your answers show that you are putting out some serious effort. Keep it going!"

"A good student like you shows even more of the same ideas. Please give me two more examples."

"You are well on your way."

"Your comments in class tell me that you know this stuff even better than you wrote. All you need to do is write a few sentences just like you talk. See me after class and we will work on how to write your excellent thoughts even better."

"Your answers show that you are really getting there. A little more on (specify) would make it even better. Keep it up!"

Realize that the comments above place the emphasis more on "effort" than on "achievement." Achievement is most apt to occur when students believe that how they do is directly linked to the amount of effort they put forth. By the way, educators are much more likely to get better results when sharing these thoughts privately with difficult students. Keep in mind that many difficult students do not consider themselves worthy of positive feedback. When they hear positive comments, it is incongruent with the negative beliefs they have about themselves. The discomfort this creates can lead many students to retreat to their inappropriate behavior. Other difficult students believe

that they have to be bad to appeal favorably to their peers. If positive comments are offered in public, they become concerned about losing the "respect" of their peers. For these reasons, educators are much more likely to get better results when **privately** sharing the kinds of positive comments offered above.

PUT THE RESPONSIBILITY ON YOUR STUDENTS FOR CHOICES THEY MAY LATER REGRET – A big problem faced by numerous educators is the blame that is placed on them by students who do not take responsibility for their actions, and their parents. It gets tiring to hear about how missing homework assignments are due to the teacher's negligence or how a poor grade on the test is due to the teacher not having taught the material. From a troubled student's perspective, landing in the office for disciplinary action is the result of a "set-up" by either the teacher or another student. Many of these blaming complaints can be prevented by having students immediately accountable for the consequences that happen to them.

For example, when students do not do their homework, have them write their excuse on an index card. Put the dated cards in the student's portfolio so that it is available at the next parent-teacher conference. If you give

students opportunities to improve their grades by either staying after school for extra help, revising the assignment or re-taking the test (and they do none of the above), require them to write a sentence or two acknowledging their choice (i.e. "Mrs. Hahn gave me three opportunities to improve my grade on the test and I decided against doing any of them"). Be sure that the statement is dated and then placed in the student's portfolio. These types of procedures can teach your students powerful lessons about responsibility while reducing parental excusing and enabling.

REFER TO THEIR CHILD AS "OUR CHILD"– Whenever you speak to a parent, talk about "our" child. For example, Ms. Jones calls with concerns about Jamie's low achievement in your class. Listen to her concerns. When the time comes for problem solving, ask, "What do you think we can do to help Jamie do even better. I look forward to helping our young man in any way I can."

CONSULT WITH OTHER STAFF WHO KNOW THE FAMILY FOR SUGGESTIONS – Ask around school to see who might know a challenging parent or family. Chances are you are not alone!! Touch base with faculty who can

provide some insight and who might be able to offer suggestions about how to most effectively communicate. For example, another teacher may have previously found that Mrs. Santos is a very caring person but with a harsh exterior that can feel intimidating. Since harshness can often shut down communication, having such knowledge can help the educator stay focused on the issue without becoming defensive. You can seek suggestions informally or more formally at a faculty meeting. Don't be afraid to ask other teachers who have had the student of concern about what has worked for them to improve the student's behavior or gain better parental cooperation. It can also be helpful to frame the issue in more general terms so that faculty might benefit from each other's ideas. Suggest that a faculty meeting be devoted to sharing helpful ways of gaining cooperation from "resistant" parents. All teachers are invited to share specific strategies that have worked at least some of the time.

STRATEGIES THAT PROVIDE SUPPORT & ADVICE FOR PARENTS

Many difficult parents are themselves struggling to guide and raise their challenging children. This section offers numerous tips to share with parents that can help with everyday practical challenges of parenting such as how to give commands effectively to get your kids to do what you want. As well, specific methods are offered that parents can use to promote desired traits in their children such as how to become a responsible person. All of these strategies are designed to offer helpful guidance for parents. When difficult parents understand that their child's teacher understands what they are going through and can offer some helpful tools, home-school cooperation is deeply enhanced.

UNDERSTAND WHAT THEY ARE UP AGAINST – Nagging, whining and complaining children can be formidable foes for both educator and parent. It is often easier in the short-run for parents to look the other way when concerns about their child's behavior are brought to their

attention. It can help for us to let parents know that most children are quite gifted in whining their way to what they want. As noted in another section, informal surveys of teenagers found that most expect to ask for what they want _nine times_ before getting it. Similarly, most youngsters probably expect that they will need to gripe at least nine times before their parent comes to the rescue and holds an "unfair" teacher accountable for whatever misery is being caused. The bottom line is that today's youth are entirely prepared to endlessly persist in wearing their parents down in order to get what they want.

Parents need to learn to say no without guilt. We can help by sharing information such as this with them. Expressing your understanding of this phenomenon will often help in assisting parents to deal with their children more effectively. You might say to the parent,

"I know you have concerns about how things are going in class and I want to get to that. But first, I have noticed that most youngsters nowadays can be quite persistent when they know what they want. I have also noticed that many can get quite angry when they don't get what they think they deserve. Mary can be strong about wanting things her way. How do you handle Mary's persistence at home?"

Together, we must be consistent in holding students to high expectations, even when that may make parents and educators unpopular. Indulged children become self-centered and are at greater risk for indulging at-risk behaviors such as drug and alcohol abuse.

HELP PARENTS LEARN TO REWARD THEIR CHILDREN WITHOUT BUYING THINGS – Too many children and students expect to be tangibly rewarded for effort or achievement. They learn that an activity only has worth if there is a pay-off. Yet true success in school as in life is accomplished through such values as hard work, honesty, caring about others and delaying gratification. Many parents appreciate learning or being reminded of ways that they can reinforce these values on a daily basis.

WAYS OF REWARDING CHILDREN THAT COST NO MONEY

1. Show excitement in your child's discoveries
2. Acknowledge their insights in a conversation
3. Notice an act of self-sacrifice
4. Ask for their opinion
5. Listen to their experiences and stories

Kids feel really good when they are noticed for a thoughtful action that they did for others – it could be as simple as helping to carry in the groceries or as consuming as befriending a senior citizen. Remind parents at every opportunity to show excitement in their children's discoveries, acknowledge their insights in a conversation, notice an act of self-sacrifice, ask for an opinion and listen to their experiences and stories. Although such moments won't completely eliminate cravings for the hottest product in our extremely materialistic culture, they will help place a premium on the values that lead to real success and accomplishment.

TEACH PARENTS HOW TO GIVE THEIR CHILDREN EFFECTIVE COMMANDS – Many parents who come across as angry are actually quite frustrated at their own inability to get their children to comply at home. Problems at school are usually symptomatic of problems that parents have in gaining their child's compliance at home. With a small percentage of parents, it is impossible to get to a point in our relationship where they acknowledge problems at home. However, most parents are searching for a listening ear, and if the teacher offers sufficient empathy and understanding, most parents become open

to sharing their own concerns. There are some effective tips we can offer when parents share frustrations around the problem of gaining compliance from their children at home. There are specific characteristics that can make commands effective.

- They should be directly stated, specific and consist of one step.
- They should be developmentally appropriate, phrased positively when possible and presented one at a time.
- Approximately five-seconds between commands is minimum.
- Verbal praise is offered after giving the command followed by a display of appreciation after compliance has been achieved.

A few examples follow:

> **"Joey, your room needs cleaning. Thanks."**

After compliance,

> **"Wow Joey, I especially like the way you put your shoes away."**

> *"Martha, we use our words when we are mad, not our fists. Thanks for using your grown-up words like PLEASE STOP."*

After compliance,

> *"I am so proud Martha at how well you used your*

grown up words when Jeffrey interrupted your game without asking."

"Emily, I care too much to allow you to ride in Sally's car with a broken headlight. You can either allow me to drive you to the party, not go or you can get another ride in a safe car."

After compliance,

"I appreciate your willingness to use good judgment last night by choosing a safe option."

THANK PARENTS FOR THEIR COOPERATION BEFORE YOU GET IT – Compliance and cooperation dramatically improves when appreciation is expressed before the cooperative act occurs. Thank a challenging person for doing what you ask before he actually does it. Think about it. Imagine that your principal asks you to do something unpleasant but thanks you in advance. For example,

"Mrs. Smith, we are struggling to get security at the basketball game. I am sure you are busy but would we ever appreciate you helping out."

As much as you might prefer to say no, it becomes quite difficult to do so. You ask your child,

"Steve, company is coming over tonight. Thanks so

much for straightening your room this morning. It means a lot to me."

Try this with difficult parents when you want or need their involvement in a way that might be difficult for them. For example,

"Ms. Lewis, Bobby could really use a few extra minutes of reading practice and I really appreciate you sacrificing your time to help him out. I know both he and I can count on you. He is a lucky boy. Thanks so much. Incidentally, please call tomorrow and let me know how it went."

- **Identify** exactly what you want parents to do to support your efforts in helping their child (i.e. "It would be really helpful if you _____," or "I know Billy (child) and I can both count on you doing _____").

- **Express your appreciation** for the action (i.e. "Thanks so much for this important support that will help your child be successful").

- **Evaluate the result** (i.e. "I'll plan to call back tomorrow to let you know how it went. Thanks.").

It can be very helpful to teach parents this method of gaining cooperation when they struggle to get compliance from their children.

USE LANGUAGE THAT BUILDS SUCCESS – Although parents of successful students can be demanding and challenging, at least we can applaud their efforts in supporting their children even when that creates more stress for us. Every teacher's goal should be to do whatever it takes to facilitate student success. Naturally, there are limits. We cannot do their homework or take tests for them. But there are many small things that we can say and do every day that can keep our students motivated and their difficult parents satisfied or at least at bay.

Teach the parents of your students how to encourage their children. Give them examples of things you do and say that are usually motivating to your students. Try saying at least one of the following comments every day to each of your challenging students for at least two weeks and encourage parents to do the same:

"You are making my day by working as well as you are."

"You hung in there even though the work was hard. I am impressed."

"Your effort paid off. Congratulations."

"Keep up the good work."

"Strange as this may sound, your mistake (behavior) helps me understand that I need to explain this more

clearly. I bet others were confused as well. Thanks for the help."

"Your improvement is a joy to see. Keep it up."

This is one terrific effort!"

"Looks like getting here on time is really helping. I notice your grades improving."

"I am one lucky teacher (parent) to have a student (child) who_____."

"Wow, the progress I saw today when you did_____ is really neat."

"Way to go!"

"Awesome. Give yourself five."

"Showing up took a lot. Thanks."

"You made my day today."

"That may not be the best grade, but you have a lot to be proud of and I hope you are."

"(Name of the student/child), you are one of the main reasons I enjoy teaching/being a parent."

FOCUS PARENTS ON HOW TO TEACH THEIR CHILDREN RESPONSIBILITY

– Responsibility requires that individuals believe that the things that happen to them are mostly and often a result of their own actions. You are late for an appointment because you decided to stop at a store to squeeze in one last errand and then had to wait on line unexpectedly long to pay your bill. Because you were late, you miss your appointment, and you have to reschedule for next week. If you attribute your lateness to your own poor planning (leaving your house later than you should) and the consequence to your own decision-making (trying to squeeze in another errand), you are likely to quickly learn not to make the same mistake again. However, if you are rescued from your mistake (earlier appointments are backed up and your lateness has no consequence), you are more likely to repeat it. When individuals are responsible for what happens to them in any given situation, they develop an "internal locus of control." If you believe that forces outside your control cause things to happen, you have an "external locus of control." This results in excuse-making such as IT'S NOT MY FAULT; HE DID IT FIRST; IT JUST BROKE. Responsibility means teaching children that their actions cause results. There are three skills associated with developing an internal orientation – predicting, choosing and planning.

1. PREDICTING STRATEGIES – In order to be responsible, children need to understand that certain behaviors bring predictable results. If children can make no connection between what they do and what happens next, then no learning can occur. Life becomes a game of chance. Predictability comes from consistency. If you say you will do something, do it. Keep your promises. Keep things on schedule. If you say to your continually late awakening teenager who you have already rescued more than once that he will have to make his own plans to get to school if he misses the bus, follow through. Don't give him a ride. Teaching a forgetful child to bring materials to school is better accomplished by allowing her to experience the school consequences of being unprepared rather than running to school carrying the forgotten book bag. Show parents how to ask their children lots of predicting questions:

What do you think will happen if you don't get your assignment completed?

What do you think your teacher would say if you gave her a compliment?

How do you think your brother would react if you offered to share your ipod?

What are some consequences that could happen if you keep picking on other kids?

2. CHOOSING STRATEGIES – In order to learn responsibility, children must have more than one real choice. In raising children, "do it my way or else" has a place, but is not a real choice. When children are given real choices, there is no guarantee they will want any of them, but it is a beginning for learning how to be responsible. Give parents examples of how they can give real choices to teach responsibility:

You can clean up your mess right now or you can do it in a half-hour.

When you are angry, you can tell how you feel or write a note.

You can eat what I cook or you can cook dinner.

You can do the laundry or mow the lawn. It's up to you.

You can get your homework done before your favorite show or after.

3. PLANNING STRATEGIES – The better you are able to plan, the more likely you are to control what happens to

you. Shopping lists, recipes, maps, directions and budgets are all ways of planning how to get what we want or where we go. A plan usually has a series of steps that need to be followed in order for a desired result to occur. Parents can teach this important skill by asking appropriate questions. For example:

John, how can you earn enough money to buy that new video game you want?

Seems to me that if you work all those hours to earn enough, there may not be enough time to keep your grades up at school. What are you going to do about that?

*That solution won't work for me because_____.
Let's think about one that could work for both of us. What are some of your ideas?*

If you worried about that now rather than later, what would you do?

ENCOURAGE PARENTS TO TALK WITH THEIR CHILDREN ABOUT CLASSROOM LEARNING – Mapp and Henderson (2002) point out that high-achieving students from all backgrounds have parents who encourage them, talk with them about school, keep them focused on learning and

homework, and help them plan for higher education. It seems that whether they are discussing books, preparing for tests or projects, or helping with homework, parent involvement is a key factor in raising achievement.

To help facilitate parent involvement with their children about classroom learning, prepare a suggestion sheet that parents can use. Suggested questions to guide discussion are:

What did you learn today?

Tell me two of the easiest assignments your teacher(s) gave you today.

What was most challenging about your class(es) today?

When you were unsure about something at school today, what did you do?

What happened next?

What are some of the things from today's class that you think might be on the next test?

Which part of your homework do you expect to do first?

If your teacher could get you to be a little better at one thing, what do you think she would suggest?

ENCOURAGE PARENTS TO HAVE MEALS WITH THEIR CHILDREN AND SHUT OFF THE TV

ENCOURAGE PARENTS TO HAVE MEALS WITH THEIR CHILDREN AND SHUT OFF THE TV – In our busy bordering on crazed societal pace, family dinners have become more the exception than the norm. Various surveys find that only one in three families eat together every day. Even more startling is that of those who eat together, the vast majority report having the television on in the background. The success of our students largely depends upon parental involvement and interest in their education. The reality is that all people have to eat and it can be during this time that focused, distraction-free time can be given. A sit-down meal can be a wonderful opportunity for children to learn social skills, conversational skills and table manners. Be respectful of differences among families while suggesting gradual increases in distraction-free family meals with the television off.

STRATEGIES FOR HANDLING DIFFICULT MOMENTS WITH PARENTS

This section provides strategies to use when parents complain, blame, criticize or go over your head. In addition, specific methods are suggested to gain cooperation from difficult parents when students are misbehaving. Numerous strategies that show how to defuse angry parents are offered. Finally, practical ways are described to gain administrative support while working with difficult parents and their children.

PUT YOURSELF IN THEIR SHOES – Try to put yourself at the receiving end of what you are about to share with a parent. If it was your child in trouble, how would you want the teacher to talk to you? What would you want to hear about your child? If it was true but all negative, how would you react? What would you want the teacher to know about your child? When a student concerns you, how can you ask questions of a parent to get important information? Bottom line: speak to parents the same way you would want to be spoken with if it was your child.

Most difficult parents are better able to handle criticism when they believe you care about their child and that you recognize his strengths as well as behaviors that need improvement.

THINK OF YOURSELF AS THE AMATEUR AND THE PARENT AS THE PRO – Keep yourself open to the idea

that parents, no matter how challenging, might have a lot to offer regarding how to best help their child. Be open to hearing from them. Make one of your goals to gain their perspective on how you can help their child. Ask engaging questions like,

> *"At home, what are some things that Joey likes to do?"*
>
> **"Most kids, including my own, don't always do what we want. When Joey is determined to do his own thing and you do not approve, what usually happens next?"**
>
> *"Are there ever times that Joey refuses to do what you ask? What do you do then?"*

If you are a parent, show some vulnerability here. For example,

> *"One of my children at home sometimes says or does things that I don't like and I have found _____ (describe the way that worked best) while not perfect, is better than doing ____(describe a way that works*

*poorly and you suspect the parent may be doing).
What do you find with your child?"*

If you are not a parent, offer something like,

*"Kids react differently to rules. Some are easier to guide
than others. I sometimes struggle to know the right
thing with all of my students. How is it for you at home
with Ava?"*

STAY FIRM WHEN VALUES ARE CHALLENGED –

When parents challenge or accuse, stay focused on the
values you are supporting. Nothing undermines classroom discipline more than backing down on what is
educationally sound in the name of doing what is "politically correct." I recall a case involving the temporary
suspension of a coach who held a few sports practices at
the school bus garage, having his players cleaning buses
after an incident in which some of the team made a mess
of the bus while en route to a contest. The suspension of
the coach followed complaints of group punishment by
a few parents. Clearly, the coach was upholding the value
that we sink or swim together as a team and that a team is
accountable for all its members. His choice to have them
clean buses was also a logical consequence of the behavior. He should have been praised for this thoughtful ac-

tion rather than put through such stress.

While we live in a culture that has too often gone too far in the direction of supporting individual rights to the exclusion of group responsibility, it is incumbent upon each of us to identify and then uphold the values that we know are necessary for good learning and teaching to occur.

STRATEGIZE WITH ADMINISTRATION AND/OR SPECIAL AREA EDUCATOR WHEN A PARENT COMPLAINS – It is certainly difficult to anticipate all of the factors that may lead to parental dissatisfaction. However, when a parent initiates a complaint directly to you and you feel unable to resolve the complaint in a manner that seems satisfactory to the parent, inform your administrator and/or a trusted colleague at your earliest convenience. Tell the administrator what happened and the specifics that led to parental dissatisfaction. Explain that despite your direct efforts, you were unable to feel that the matter was satisfactorily resolved and why. It is then wise to brainstorm possible next steps with the administrator. You might suggest that the administrator call to explain his knowledge of the situation along with your concern about it while exploring what might be done. You could ask the admin-

istrator to make herself available for a three-way conference in a mediator role that might lead to a resolution of
the issue. You might just simply ask the administrator for
advice as to how to best proceed from here.

Try not to wait for the parent to contact the administrator. When you have disagreed with a parent while
believing that you are upholding a position that is educationally sound, initiate contact with your administrator and express your perspective in a confident, proactive
manner while keeping open to a possible way of solving
the problem that you hadn't considered.

COMMUNICATE YOUR THOUGHTS CLEARLY – Be clear in
letting parents know what you want and expect. Knowing what you want means clearly expressing what you can
or will do to help your students be successful and learn
about responsibility. Openly sharing our wants and needs
sets the stage to engage in joint problem-solving, so that
decisions are more often based on cooperation between
educators and parents. The language we use can be the
difference between alienating a parent or eliciting cooperation. Examples of "opening" language we can use to
communicate our thoughts clearly and gain cooperation

from parents follow:

"I believe what will help (student's name) be most successful is_____."

"From my point of view, it is especially important to _____."

"I am open to ideas that will help (student's name) learn to be even more independent. Do you have any suggestions?"

"I am excited to see that when we do_____, (student's name) experiences more success."

"I'm not sure of the best solution, but what makes most sense to me is_____."

"It is my hope that we can work closely together to make sure (student's name) has a great year."

All of these "openers" can be followed with,

"What are your thoughts about that?"

SET LIMITS WHEN NECESSARY BUT STAY OPEN TO OTHER WAYS – Keep being guided by your main goals: helping students be successful and teaching them important life lessons about responsibility. When students break rules that require a meeting with parents, stay focused on these goals, but keep an open mind to parental sugges-

tions that could achieve the same goals with more student or parent support. For example,

"If I understand your concerns correctly, you think it is very important for Samantha to be active during recess so that she can better concentrate when she is in her seat. I'm all for that. My view about keeping Samantha in the classroom during recess is to give her some extra time to get her work done. Let's see if we can think of some other ways that might give her the activity she needs while making sure that her work gets done. I'm thinking she could do it at home under your supervision, work in class with another student or continue to do it during recess and have more activity at home. How do these ideas sound? How do you see it?"

After some possible solutions are discussed you might conclude,

Now that I know of your concerns, I'm thinking that maybe I ought to meet with Samantha and see what she thinks of these solutions.

DON'T TAKE OFFENSIVE BEHAVIOR PERSONALLY –

Many times in seminars I teach, educators acknowledge how much they struggle to keep their anger in check when students and parents say or do offensive things. I have stated many times in many forums that these days,

an effective educator needs a touch of "multiple personality disorder." A full-blown case is obviously undesirable, because a person would no longer know his own identity. But a "touch" is a good thing because while it is natural to want to "knee-jerk" react when our buttons are pushed and fight back, being a professional educator means stopping and thinking before acting (what we try to teach students with self-control issues all the time).

Take a step back and a deep breath before reacting. Realize that an angry parent is advocating for her child and while you aren't a punching bag for the parent's frustration and will not accept disrespectful treatment, try to calm yourself before you choose your response to the parent. For example, if you hear words that you find offensive or are being accused of something you know you didn't do, try to hear the message as if it is neutral or even silly. If someone called you "Spiderman", it is unlikely that you would take the comment seriously. If you had been angrily accused of causing World War II, you hopefully would feel concern for the accuser's poor reality testing. Try to stay personally connected without taking offensive behavior personally. Once you defuse yourself, you will remain in charge during the conference, which will enable you to think clearly and act with purpose.

AGREE WITH THE ACCUSATION BY ACKNOWLEDGING ITS LEGITIMACY EVEN WHEN YOU PERSONALLY DISAGREE

One of the quickest ways to redirect the flow of communication when verbally attacked is by agreeing with whatever is said. There may be some truth to the accusation, but even if there isn't, there is nothing to be gained by arguing. Remember, the goal should be having an angry or unhappy parent leave the conference being more supportive of what you are doing to help their child be successful and responsible. For example, Pete's father, Mr. Greco initiates contact with his teacher or responds to a request for a conference by blaming. He says,

"Pete tells me that he is very bored in your class. What are you going to do to be more interesting?"

With the goal to defuse, a good response is,

"There is probably some truth to what he says. In fact, it is always my goal to be more interesting, and if either he or you have any ideas about how that would work for him, I would love to hear."

It is best to conclude with,

"Bored or not, I'm sure you agree that we need to help Pete find better ways to express himself when he is unhappy."

Offer examples of more proper ways to express frustration or unhappiness.

There is a much better chance of keeping the focus on ways to help the student improve when we acknowledge and agree with complaints we receive.

GIVE PARENTS A CHANCE TO INTERVENE BEFORE YOU TAKE OTHER ACTION – Give parents a chance to influence their children before sending students to the office or the guidance counselor for a disciplinary intervention. Let the parent(s) know that there recently have been some difficulties caused by their child's behavior that are getting beyond your control. Call home or invite parents in for a conference. ***Start your conversation by thanking*** them for coming or giving you the time to discuss their child. Try to begin on a positive note (i.e. "Thanks for coming in today. I want to start by saying how pleased I have been with Glen's work habits. He has been prepared with his work and often participates in class"). ***Proceed by identifying the current problem*** ("Glen has been having some trouble these last few days using proper language and when I remind him, he has been getting angry and argumentative"). The next step is to let parents know that they are an ***alternative to a corrective plan and request their***

assistance ("I've been thinking about writing referrals for disciplinary action and asking his counselor to meet with him, but I first wanted to ask for your assistance"). Finally, **_be specific_** about the kind of assistance you want ("Can I can count on getting your help in discussing this with him and making sure he remembers to use proper language"). If a willingness to cooperate is expressed, _**conclude by thanking the parent and setting a time for follow-up**_ ("I appreciate your help on this. After you talk to him, I would especially like to know how I might be able to help. Please call me by Thursday and let me know how your conversation went").

REFRAME THE PARENT — It can be just as helpful and effective to view a difficult parent as a glass that is half full. As mentioned earlier, as unpleasant as a difficult parent can be, we can at least be thankful that he is advocating on behalf of his child. Try to picture a difficult parent as a grizzly bear or mother lion protecting her cub. Perhaps the cub needs no protection because nobody means to do it harm. Does the mother know this? More than likely, she errs on the side of caution and scares off or possibly attacks even harmless intruders.

Being a parent often feels like walking a tightrope of

confusion while trying to figure out when to support and when to let go. Try to see your excuse making, enabling parents as mothers or fathers protecting their precious cubs. Although they may not be doing their children any favors in the long run, they are unlikely to surrender this protective role prematurely because of the perceived danger. They must first trust that you are on their side before they welcome you into their den, and that requires finding as many ways as you can to let them know that their child's success is as important to you as it is to them.

HAVE STUDENTS CALL THEIR PARENTS — In most cases that require contacting a parent to discuss inappropriate behavior, it is most powerful and memorable to have the student make the call. The teacher should be present when the student calls her parent at home or at work. Ideally, the conversation should occur via speakerphone so that you can hear and when necessary participate in the proceedings. Younger children may lack the necessary sophistication of language, so we can provide cues, prompts and even scripts. Clyde Hill elementary school in the Seattle area created a script (*figure 3*) that children can follow when parental contact is needed. A few adaptations have been included.

FIGURE 3

CLYDE ELEMENTARY SCHOOL STUDENT SCRIPT FOR TELEPHONE CALL TO PARENT

Hello (Mom or Dad), this is (student's name).

I was asked to call you because I _____.

Mrs._____ (teacher) is sitting next to me right now and is listening to our conversation. What I did is against the rules and I was asked to talk with you about my decision to do this. The thing that I did wrong was_ _____. The reason it is wrong is_____ _____. I learned_____ _____.

Next time I will_____.

I will talk more with you about this when I get home, and I will make a better effort today to follow the school rules. Is there anything you want to say to my teacher or me before I say good-bye?

APOLOGIZE WHEN YOU HAVE MADE A MISTAKE –

When you blow it and know it, apologize. For example, "Charkendra, I lost my patience with you earlier and I am sorry about some of the things I said. That wasn't right of me." Adding apologizing to the mix of how we behave with our students conveys honesty and defines us as thoughtful and approachable. In fact, teachers who communicate openly with their students rarely have problems with parents.

For parents who are especially touchy or when you know that a student continually complains about everything to his parent, it is wise to contact difficult parents

before they come loaded for bear. For example, "Ms. Samuels, there was an incident at school today in which some items turned up missing. I mistakenly thought it was Hiram who was responsible and asked him about this. He became a little upset and although things seem fine, I just wanted to touch base with you and let you know what happened." It is usually a good idea to conclude with something positive (i.e. "Incidentally, Hiram has really been making progress with his writing. Have you noticed this as well?").

APOLOGIZE AFTER BEING ACCUSED EVEN IF YOU DON'T THINK YOU DID ANYTHING WRONG – One of the best ways to defuse an angry parent who has a hard time being rational, is to apologize for all of your perceived wrongdoings. First, try a rational approach. Explain your perspective. But if this gets you nowhere after three attempts, don't try to change the parent's mind. Since you are unlikely to convince the parent of your perspective, act as if you made a mistake and offer to work harder. For example, "Gee Mr. Lopez, I am very sorry that you and Carlos (your son) feel as strongly as you do. In no way is it my desire to either lose him as a student or lose your support as a parent. I will obviously need to work harder

to gain your trust and I plan to do just that. Thanks for letting me know some of the things you would like to see me do." Apologizing in this manner takes a lot less time than trying to explain facts or circumstances to somebody whose primary interest is conflict.

ACTIVELY LISTEN TO ALL CONCERNS – The most important skill to develop in life is the ability to listen to others and then letting them know that you captured the essence of both their content and their feelings. Successful candidates for jobs usually do more listening to the interviewer than sharing information about themselves. The first step is to put away what you want to say so that you can really hear what somebody else is trying to tell you. This can be very difficult to do for many reasons including lack of time and the desire to be sure that you have said all that you wanted. Parents will hear your concerns much more clearly and less defensively when they feel that you truly understand their perspective. It is therefore very important to learn and practice the art of paraphrasing. After you hear somebody express a thought or feeling, try paraphrasing what was just said. Examples are as follows:

"What you are saying is.........................."

"If I understand, you are saying (feeling)..............."

"Wow, if I hear you correctly, your point is….."

"You seem to be thinking (feeling)……."

"If I hear you correctly, you are telling that………"

"How (exciting, frustrating, annoying) it must be when…………….."

Being a great listener means going beyond the content. Try giving feedback that gets at the parent's feelings:

"It must be difficult when Billy comes home unhappy."

"Sounds like you are in a tough spot. On the one hand……but on the other…….."

"Wow, seems like you are between a rock and a hard place…….."

"Oh my gosh, you must feel……….."

"It comes across like you are feeling……………"

When you are at a loss and the words just aren't flowing, keep communication flowing with the parent. Use simple words like **WOW**, **REALLY**, and **I SEE** accompanied by caring body language conveyed with eye contact and a friendly look.

DEVELOP A CONTRACT EITHER WITH THE PARENT ALONE OR INCLUDING THE STUDENT – Contracts can be

very effective tools to get everyone on the same page. The goal is for two or more parties to a conflict to get together,

discuss concerns, share expectations and come to a satisfactory agreement. The most effective contracts require ownership of the problem by all parties along with suggestions about what each can and will do. Specific tasks are outlined for each person to ensure a positive change in the student's behavior with a means to assess the effectiveness of the plan. Contracts can be facilitated by the teacher alone or by a more neutral third party who has less emotional baggage. Typically a teacher-led contract would begin with an invitation to parents for a face-to-face meeting. The first step is often on the phone:

"Ms. Jones, I have some ideas that I would like to share that I think will help Sarah be more successful in class. I know you have some ideas as well. So I would like us to get together to share these ideas and see what makes sense to do that will best help her. I have some time either after school today or tomorrow. Which time would work best for you?"

If there is resistance or reluctance to meet, take more ownership. For example,

"I've been thinking that I must not be doing nearly as good of a job for Sarah as I would like, because if I was, I am sure that she would behave in a more cooperative way in class and you would feel better about

how things are going. I want to get together with you to find ways that I can get her best effort. Which time would work best for you?"

If the parent starts blaming, do some good reflective listening (i.e. "Sounds like you have some concerns of your own to share which are very important for me to hear. Let's figure out a time to get together.")

When you see the parent(s), it is very important to first welcome her, then state the problem while staying open to hearing about things you may be doing or not doing that the parent believes could be contributing to the problem. Propose a framework for success:

"My goal in getting together is to explore what everybody can do to help Sarah be more successful. First, I want to share my concern along with why I think it is a problem. I am eager to hear your thoughts as well so that we can explore some solutions that we agree are the best ways to help Sarah do her best."

When sharing the problem as you see it, be sure to keep the focus either on how it creates a problem for you as a teacher, how it creates a problem for other students or how it creates a problem for the targeted student. For example,

"When Sarah cuts class it becomes impossible for

her to handle this material because each day of learning leads to the next. When she misses class she falls further behind. Unfortunately, given her schedule and mine, there simply isn't enough time for her to catch up. That worries me."

The next step is to invite the parent(s) to broaden your understanding of the problem. For example,

"Most students who cut class either believe that they cannot be successful so why bother coming, while others don't show because they are trying hard to make friends and think it is cool to impress some peers by being brave enough to break important rules. A few who don't show are letting us know they are angry and feeling misunderstood. There have been some situations where students cut class because drugs or alcohol have gotten them to stop thinking about what is really important. I'm trying to understand things from Sarah's perspective and I'm wondering if you have any knowledge or hunches that could help?"

The discussion next proceeds based upon the type of information shared by the parent. If both you and the parent(s) remain genuinely uncertain about cause, begin brainstorming some "next steps" that can be evaluated over the next week or two.

FIGURE 4

SPECIFIC STEPS IN DEVELOPING A CONTRACT

A. Invite parent(s) for a face to face meeting.

B. Welcome the parent (and student) by expressing appreciation that they are there. State the problem as you see it.

C. Acknowledge that there may be some things that you are doing that could be contributing.

D. Ask parent(s) to broaden your understanding of the problem.

E. When appropriate, have other school professionals offer thoughts and share concerns.

F. Brainstorm possible solutions with the parent(s). Develop a specific plan that is agreeable and workable to both teacher and parent(s) with a time-limited horizon for evaluation.

G. Evaluate the effectiveness of the plan.

H. Go back to the drawing board if problems persist.

I. When appropriate, directly involve the student and/or other staff who might be able to help.

For example,

"From what I am hearing today, let's assume that Sarah is cutting because she believes she cannot be successful. How about I meet with her, share my concerns and offer extra help either directly or through the resource center. I would like you to monitor her homework for the next two weeks to be certain that all

assignments are complete. I am going to ask Mr. Phillips, our attendance officer, to call you at least twice a week with an update so that you know whether or not she is attending. In two weeks, I think it would make sense for us to meet again. Is this a plan that makes sense to you?"

Keep the door open to change so that parents feel they can actively contribute. Collaboration is the key. View your suggestions as hunches rather than facts.

When necessary, call for a meeting that involves the student as well as all key staff who are either part of the problem or have a possible role in the solution. Similar steps as those outlined above apply. *Figure 4* summarizes the key steps in developing a contract and *figure 5* offers an example of a comprehensive contract that involves key school personnel, parent(s) and usually the student to help a student change behavior.

SET LIMITS WITH PARENTS WHEN THEY OVERSTEP YOUR BOUNDARY — We all have our limits and when yours are reached, it is necessary and appropriate to assert yourself in a clear, no-nonsense, respectful manner. Keep in mind that people who are the least deserving of respect are often the most in need of it. Most people become less

FIGURE 5

A COMPREHENSIVE CONTRACT

1. Jamal agrees to solve problems peacefully. If angry, he will first take a few deep breaths and remind himself that fighting gets him into trouble and isn't worth the hassle.

2. If Jamal needs to get away from someone in the classroom who is bugging him, he will give Ms. Smith (teacher) a hand signal to let her know that he needs to move away.

3. If Jamal feels a wave of anger come on that he believes he cannot control, he can leave class and go right to Mr. Jones, (Guidance Counselor) for a few minutes of "chill out" time. Two trips each day is the maximum.

4. If Mr. Jones is unavailable, Jamal can sit alone in the guidance office for a few minutes. If he feels that he needs to talk things over right away, he can ask to see Mr. Ragusa (Administrator).

5. Mr. Jones will monitor this plan and report to everybody about its effectiveness at the end of the week for the first four weeks.

Student's signature

Parent signature

Teacher signature

Administrator signature

Counselor signature

angry when they feel respected. When parents are angry, try to view them as misguided advocates for their child. While you may disagree with how they are expressing themselves, we can probably all appreciate parents who advocate for their children. One of the best ways to defuse an angry parent is to acknowledge their anger as a message of support for their child. We can respect their support if not their means of expression. The following procedures can be very effective in defusing an angry parent. Use as many or as few as necessary:

1. **Acknowledge their perspective and ask for feedback**— *"Wow, Mrs. Brown, I had no idea how angry you would be. If I understand things correctly, you are particularly upset about the consequences Livan received for fighting. Am I right about that?"*

2. **Agree that there may be other ways to solve the problem** – *"Not everybody agrees with each other. If you have other ideas that can make things better, I hope you will share your thoughts before you leave."*

3. **Set limits when your boundaries are crossed** – *"I need to let you know that while I want to hear your ideas, it is not okay that you raise your voice and swear. I don't talk to parents or students in that way and I expect to be spoken to respectfully as well. Now what is it*

101

that you want to tell me?"

4. <u>**Be honest about what you can do and what you can't**</u>
   – "I think it is very important that no matter how upset Livan gets, we all let him know that at school it is never okay to fight to solve problems. School is a place for learning and neither Livan nor any of my other students are going to be able to learn if they are thinking about, planning or actually fighting. Please do not ask that I excuse his behavior even if somebody else started it."

5. <u>**Remind the parent that you are always guided by success and responsibility, not by comparing students**</u> –If parents ever want to compare your actions toward their child with another, refuse to make these comparisons. *"Mrs. Brown, I am not at liberty to tell you why I might have used a different consequence with another child. I consider that to be a private matter between myself, that child and his family. My goal is always to help each of my students become more successful and learn more about responsibility. I decided that this was the best thing to do for your child. But I'm certainly far from perfect and there may well be a better way in the future. In fact, perhaps you can help me understand what would be most helpful to support your child in becoming more successful. If you have any*

thoughts about how your child might learn better from a different consequence, I am happy to listen."

6. <u>**Offer a third party if there is a stalemate or if the parent is excessively offensive**</u> – *"I don't think we are going to be able to agree on this"* OR ***"I will not be spoken to in this way. I think Mrs. Donovan is a good choice to help us. Do you want to arrange an appointment or should I?"***

7. <u>**Ask the student to leave if the parent is inappropriate in the student's presence**</u> – When parents are unable to provide good role-modeling for their children, educators must. While it can often be helpful for a student to be present during a parent conference concerning his behavior, if his parents act in verbally or otherwise abusive ways, it will be necessary to ask the student to leave. Say to the student something like, *"Carlos, I need to have a private word with your parents. Please step outside."* Then deal directly with parents in one or more ways already suggested. With a very young child, try to arrange a specific place. Say to all present, ***"I think it is best if just the grown-ups keep talking right now, so I am going to call Mrs. Smith (fellow teacher that can be reached by intercom) and see if Carlos can stay with her for a few minutes while we***

talk." If there are no alternatives available, it is probably best to end the conference and try again at another time.

DON'T GOSSIP TO PARENTS OR STUDENTS ABOUT

OTHERS – If a parent or student questions your actions toward another student, avoid getting into specifics. As indicated earlier, explain that you consider whatever happened with the other student to be a private matter between yourself, the other student and her family. Acknowledge that you often do different things with different students because you want to help each become **successful** or learn more about **responsibility**. You are at liberty only to say that if you did something different with another student it was because of these reasons. Then turn the focus back on the person who is complaining. For example, *"My belief is that this was the best way with your child. Did I or did I not miss the boat with your child? Can you think of any better ways to help your child improve?"*

CALL PARENTS BACK RIGHT AWAY WHENEVER

POSSIBLE– There is little that aggravates people more than having their phone calls either ignored or responded

to much later on. When a parent calls and leaves a message, be sure to call back the same day. If that isn't possible, ask the school secretary to call on your behalf with a specific time that you will either be available or that you will return the call.

AGREE TO CHANGE ANY RULE AS LONG AS AN ACCEPTABLE ALTERNATIVE IS PROPOSED – Whenever a parent or student complains about a rule that you believe is necessary, agree to change the rule as long as they propose an alternative that is acceptable to you. The alternative must have a high likelihood of promoting responsibility and facilitating success while maintaining order and keeping the classroom safe. It is unwise to argue with parents or students about specific rules and consequences. Stay focused on **_success_**, **_responsibility_**, **_order_** and **_safety_**. Your message needs to be,

> *"Whenever there are problems in following rules, students are welcome to do_____ just as soon as they do_____."*

Educators need to stay focused on the important goals. Be unwavering when it comes to the goals and values, but flexible in considering other ways in which those goals can be achieved.

105

DO NOT ATTACK, CRITICIZE OR PUT DOWN THE CHILD –

When parents feel like failures, it is easy for them to get hurt and feel angry. Express caring, support and show interest. Do not sound like an unenthusiastic, disengaged customer service representative going through the motions. Use questions because you care and want to know as much as possible so you can be helpful. Try to learn from them. Learn what makes your students tick from their point of view. How was she as a younger child? What interests does he show at home? What kinds of things motivate the child at home? How are disciplinary situations handled? Are there any areas of frustration that parents are experiencing? Attempt to accumulate information by listening and showing interest.

CONCLUSION

It is my sincere hope that the many strategies offered throughout this book have provided and will continue to provide fellow educators with practical ways of handling tough parents. Many methods have been offered to positively influence the behavior and cooperation of belligerent or uninvolved parents. However, there are times when all the right moves still do not produce the best results. My friend and now retired teacher Howard Itkin, told of a parent whose complaints about her daughter's experience in his second grade class led to a time-consuming conference and the development of a plan that seemed to meet with everyone's approval. Howard remembered feeling very pleased and enthusiastic. The next day, the parent withdrew her daughter from the school.

Fortunately, most parents care for their children, want what is best for them and with no formal training, wind up raising productive and responsible people. The vast majority are reasonable in their dealings with others. That said, we live and teach in an era of too many dysfunctional families. If you work in the inner city, it is a rarity to see a father at a parent conference. You are dealing with many single mothers who had a first baby when they were themselves children and far too many who have had multiple babies out of wedlock without the emotional or financial resources to manage or cope. While most parents love their children and want only the best, too few in this predicament have a real understanding of the level of commitment to education at home that is needed for their children to be successful. On a recent visit with 10 year-old Victor, my son's "little" in the Big Brothers, Big Sisters program, he spontaneously said that he would never want to go to college because he wouldn't want to leave his family. When I asked this very bright boy if he knew anyone in his neighborhood who was going to college, Victor could not think of a single person. Sadly, Victor is one of many who face an uphill struggle to success because he has no community context for how education can really improve life.

In middle to upper class America, the connection between education and success is solid. Growing ever weaker is the link between school success and effort from the student. From an early age, students understand that doing well in school is important. Well intentioned parents race to live in neighborhoods with the "best" schools, somehow believing that it is really the school that makes all the difference. The primary responsibility for a child's success or failure is placed on the school rather than on harder to face issues such as effort and work ethic, family dynamics and sense of entitlement. Too willing are some parents to place blame for low achievement and poor behavior on everybody other than themselves and their child. If a child is not identified as "gifted," the school or teacher is viewed as at fault.

Within these realities it is understandable that frustration and even disgust can set in. Yet to be and remain a truly effective educator we must rise beyond the natural tendency to become disenchanted and angry when we are directly affected. We must daily and continuously view what we do as special and important because it is. We must listen and consider but not take personally unwarranted attacks.

We must do our utmost to help our students achieve success and therefore the hope for a good life especially when family and community fail to do its fair share.

Finally, we need to do what this book is about: help parents even when they avoid or provoke us, so that we can help them guide their children to become successful, responsible adults.

REFERENCES & BIBLIOGRAPHY

Canfield, J., Hansen, M.V., McPherson, J. (2004) *Chicken Soup for the Soul Cartoons for Teachers.* Deerfield Beach, FL: Health Communications Inc.

Curwin, R. and Mendler, A. (1999) *Discipline with Dignity* (rev. ed.) Alexandria, VA: Association for Supervision and Curriculum Development.

Gladwell, M. (2005) *Blink.* New York: Little Brown & Co.

Kindlon, D. (2003) *Too much of a good thing: Raising children of character in an indulgent age.* NY: Miramax Books.

Levinson, W. (1997) "Physician-Patient Communication: The Relationship with Malpractice Claims Among Primary Care Physicians and Surgeons." *Journal of the American Medical Association 277,* no. 7.

Mapp, K. and Henderson, A (2002) "A New Wave of Evidence: The Impact of School, Family, and Community Connections on Student Achievement. " ASCD *Education Update,* (Vol. 47., No. 3) March 2005.

McMahon, R.J. and Forehand, R.L. (2003) *Helping the noncompliant child: Family-based treatment for oppositional behavior* (2nd ed.). New York: Guilford Press.

Mendler, A. (2005) *Just in Time: Powerful strategies to promote positive behavior.* Bloomington, IN: Solution Tree.

Mendler, A. (2001) *Connecting with Students.* Alexandria, VA: Association of Supervision and Curriculum Development.

Mendler, A. (2000) *Motivating Students Who Don't Care.* Bloomington, IN: Solution Tree.

Mendler, A. (1997) *Power Struggles: Successful techniques for educators.* Rochester, NY: Discipline Associates.

MetLife Survey (2004) reported in *TIME* 2/21/05., Vol. 165, No. 8., pp 40-49.